P9-DMV-758

COMMENTS ON OTHER BOOKS BY PAUL PINES

My Brother's Madness

My Brother's Madness *is part thriller, part an exploration that not only describes the causes,character, and journey of mental illness, but also makes sense of it. It is ultimately a story of our own humanity*
—*Kirkus Review*

Take what pain, hope, sorrow, and madness there is in this world, pass it through the alembic of an educated sensibility and a deep, informed compassion, and you might be lucky enough to reach My Brother's Madness
— James Hollis, Jungian Analyst,
and author of *Why Good People do Bad Things*

The Tin Angel

This swift tale of murder and revenge rattled along styishly and fulfills all our expectations for high-grade suspense.
—*The New York Times Book Review.*

Superb...enough terror, suspense, and low-life atmosphere to keep the most jaded hard-boiled enthusiast happy.
—*The Washington Post*

I haven't read a grittier mystery in years, or—I suspect—a truer one.
— *NY Daily News*

The Hotel Madden Poems

Hotel Madden *is a fine and powerful book.* —William Bronk

Paul Pines' dedication to Hotel Madden Poems *describes the book as a "fugue." That's exactly what this brilliant and compelling work is...* — Lawrence Joseph, *American Book Review*

Breath

...the Poems in Breath *constitute a heartfelt, extended meditation on the transporting effects of everyday phenomena, how the psychic wormholes that allow and instantaneous travel along our internal galaxies hide just underneath the next memory, the next sentence, and behind the all, the ALL itself—unknowable, perhaps, but in Pines' poetry nearly imaginable.*

— Fred Muratori, *The American Book Review*

Adrift On Blinding Light

Pines take the reader on a mysterious complicated journey. Dreams, archetypes, icons, friends and confessions swirl through the poems in beautiful and complex images...This wonderfully unpredictable, intuitive book navigates the conscious and subconscious worlds with fluid, imaginative, and fascinating energy--as poets should do.

— William Kelly, *Multicultural Review*

Adrift on Blinding Light *is full of exquisite moments; of words and phrases that have been mined by the author like gems and presented to us with the sense of wonder they engender and deserve.*
— Lee Bellavance, *The Café Review*

Paul Pines' latest book, Adrift on Blinding Light, *offers a dazzling tour through a poet's self construction...although these images may not raise us up in the emotional sense, they always seem to arrive as a startling surprise, perfectly timed to shake us out of the ordinary.*

— Neil Kozolowicz, *Rain Taxi*

Paul Pines is a latter-day pioneer of feeling, in one verse aiming to write a poem of last words; in another finding and using the single word reverberating "through which/ to approach/ what remains unexplored." Adrift on Blinding Light *is a book of brilliant insights and lyrical sadness, and of a modest hard-headedness that will stay in the mind.*

—Corinne Robins, *The American Book Review*

Taxidancing

Reading Pines is not unlike listening to good jazz. The poems are strangely emblematic allowing us to progressively come into their world, becoming, as we go, increasingly hip and eager to hear their urgencies. — Julia Conner, *First Intensity*

What a background for a poet. Paul Pines grew up in Brooklyn, and spent time in the Lower East Side of NYC. He tended bar, drove a cab, shipped out as a merchant seaman, and opened his own jazz club in the Bowery: "The Tin Palace" in 1970. He is now a practicing psychotherapist in upstate New York. So this ain't your usual MFA-trained bard, but certainly one who has been well-schooled. Hugely Recommended.
— Doug Holder, *Boston Area Small Press and Scene*

Last call at the Tin Palace

Thank you, Paul Pines, for a sublime ride! — David Meltzer

…the poems are magical, revealing, yet personal, and all the time - engaging. Last Call at the Tin Palace delivers.
— Brian Gilmore, *JAZZ TIMES*

Last Call at the Tin Palace, *by Paul Pines…poems that are stories that are jazz that are memories that are everlasting imprints of music on retinas…*
— Bob Holman, *Poetry Picks - The Best Books of 2009*

REFLECTIONS
IN A SMOKING MIRROR

POEMS OF MEXICO & BELIZE

BY
PAUL PINES

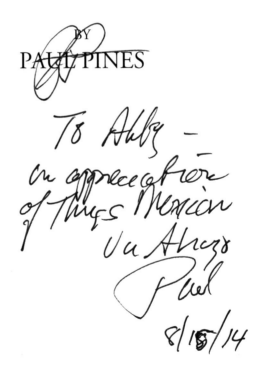

To Abby —
in appreciation
of things Mexican
Un Abrazo
Paul
8/15/14

DOS MADRES PRESS INC.

P.O.Box 294, Loveland, Ohio 45140
www.dosmadres.com   editor@dosmadres.com

Dos Madres is dedicated to the belief that the small press is essential to the vitality of contemporary literature as a carrier of the new voice, as well as the older, sometimes forgotten voices of the past. And in an ever more virtual world, to the creation of fine books pleasing to the eye and hand.

Dos Madres is named in honor of Vera Murphy and Libbie Hughes, the "Dos Madres" whose contributions have made this press possible.

Dos Madres Press, Inc. is an Ohio Not For Profit Corporation and a 501 (c) (3) qualified public charity. Contributions are tax deductible.

Executive Editor: Robert J. Murphy

Illustration & Book Design: Elizabeth H. Murphy
www.illusionstudios.net

Typset in Adobe Garamond Pro

Library of Congress Control Number: 2011932630
ISBN 978-1-933675-60-2

ACKNOWLEDGMENTS
Some of these poems have appeared in *Lillabulero, Mulch, City, First Intensity*, and *The Café Review*.
Author photo by Carol Pines

First Edition

RAISING THE VISION SERPENT

The Quiche Maya, native to Guatemala and Belize, tell us that Gucumatz unfolded blue-green wings over the smoking mirror of primal water to bring forth humans who would honor the gods, but also reflect them. The dialogue among mortals, gods and the ancestors involved raising the Vision Serpent from the smoke of burning blood-soaked bark—a metaphor for consciousness that gives new meaning to the phrase "it's all smoke and mirrors." What is called forth speaks with a foundational voice from depths that are inaccessible by ordinary means. In the case of the Quiche Maya, the voice of origin dates back to pre-Classic times, as far back as 1,000 BCE. On a stela at Tikal, Lady Xoc, a rope of blood-knots perforating her tongue, watches the founder of her line, Progenitor Jaguar, poke his head out the jaw of the serpent rising in the smoke from her blood bowl.

The long Aztec migration from their mysterious northern city of origin, Aztlan, possibly in the American Southwest, ended on the swampy banks of an island on Lake Texcoco, in Central Mexico. Here, they encountered, as prophesied, an eagle holding a serpent in its beak perched on a nopal cactus. On that spot, in 1248 AD, they built cities connected by gardens and causeways. They called the volcanic lake Smoking Mirror, which also refers to the original face of creation—where, in a time before time, the Plumed Serpent, Quetzalcóatl, violently shaped order from the dismembered parts of the matrix-monster known as The Hungry Woman, whose many mouths still cry out for blood at the heart of the creation. Hearing her wail, Aztec priests and warriors regularly shed ritual blood and petitioned the ancestors to appease her.

The Black Caribs, slaves escaped from foundered ships, transplanted West African roots to the Caribbean. Ritual dance and trance to summon ancestors have long been common in villages along the Mosquito Coast from Nicaragua through Belize. Such shamanic beliefs as practiced by the Aztec, Maya and Carib, have given way to a world driven by time instead of depth. The volcanic dark of ancestral water no longer heats the surface on which we live, or informs our psyche—the original smoking mirror. Perhaps some poets still experience it in a primal way, responding to the cry they hear at the heart of creation.

Reflections in A Smoking Mirror is a crazy quilt of historical and personal material knit by themes unraveled over the last thirty years. I first went to Mexico in the 60s, before there was a paved road between Mexico City and Yucatan, and most of the archaeological sites referred to here were still covered by bush. I went again after returning from Vietnam when the remains of lost civilizations and the legacy of conquest drove me to search for what might be reflected in the Smoking Mirror, both as volcanic lake, and metaphor. During that time I've come to understand what I may have done beyond my intention, to let let the ancestors speak in ways that have not always been apparent to me, except for the blood-smoke on these pages.

Paul Pines
Glens Falls, NY
5.10.11

TABLE OF CONTENTS

RAISING THE VISION SERPENT – xi

I - CONFIGURATIONS OF CONQUEST

Restaurant Villa Hermosa – 1
Configurations of Conquest – 2
Windsong – 5
Vectors – 7

The Moctezuma Poems – 8
    1 - Moctezuma
    2 - Of His Physical Presence
    3 - At What Point Did He Break
    4 - The Royal Fifth
    5 - Vanishing Point

Matamoros – 13
Cacamatzin's song – 14
The Concubine – 16
After a Mayan Folk Song by Antonio Medez Bolio – 18
Notes on a Glass Harmonica – 19
Zopilote at the Hotel Flamingo – 20
150th Anniversary of Mexican Independence – 21
Reflections in a Smoking Mirror – 23
Timepiece – 24
Tierra de Nakuk Pech – 25
Mother Earth – 26
Vix A Kava – 28
The Mystic Warrior – 29

II - MY NAME IS NAKUK PECH

SYNCHRONICITY – 33
My Name is Nankuk Pech – 35
Afterword – 43

III - THE BELIZE NEWS

MIRROR TRAVEL – 47
Creole – 51
What Is Buried Here – 53
Taking A Shower At The Hotel Mopan – 54
Coastwise On The Fury – 55
Dangriga – 56
Crossing the Lagoon – 57
George, The King of Rum Point – 59
Birds of Belize – 61
Rum Point Sutra – 63
Buita Banafi – 65
Augustine's Daughter – 66
The Way Things Are – 68
View From The Beach – 70
Birds of Belize II – 71
Punta Gorda – 72
The Belize News – 74

End Notes – 77
A Partial Glossary – 83

About the Author – 87

I

CONFIGURATIONS OF CONQUEST

Timelessness is found in the lapsed moments of perception, in the common pause that breaks apart into a sandstorm of pauses. The malady of wanting to "make" is "unmade," and the malady of wanting to be "able" is "disabled".

Robert Smithson,
INCIDENTS OF MIRROR TRAVEL IN THE YUCATAN

RESTAURANT VILLA HERMOSA

"Huevos revueltos
tortillas de harina
refritos y Nescafe!"

The waitress shouts my order
through a hole in the wall
of a restaurant
                    outside San Fernando

to a man in front of an open fire

and the way flames leap around him
I know he is cooking my breakfast

over the heart
of Mexico

            La Dueña,
            a beauty gone to seed,

sits by the register in a blue dress
features flickering

                with the memory
                of loveliness
                as she pins back her hair:

she knows that feelings become extinct
when we cease to use them,

how we change as creatures
once they are gone.

1

CONFIGURATIONS OF CONQUEST

They knew he was coming
with his pale skin
                        black beard and robe,
                        this Quetzalcóatl
banished long ago

knew he would return
and why–
                        that he was irresistible
                        and would arrive
                        according to prophecy
                        by water from the east

They knew he hadn't come
to devour hearts
                        blood sprinkled food
                        of Tezcatlipoca
on whose lake
called Smoking Mirror
they built their cities

This one
was not so easily satisfied

The signs were undeniable

                  Northern lights

                  Volcanic eruptions
                  that made the lake
                  around them
                  boil

2

A comet

An earthquake

Moctezuma's nerves
a quivering garden
of snakes

His sister Papantzin
returned with visions
of ruin after four days
of death-like sleep

Never was so much knowledge
of so little use

          as to proclaim a god
          where there was none

          to allow 500 men
          to seize an Empire
          of millions

Impossible to understand
unless we measure it

          by what we know today
          about conquest
          and ourselves

          that we covet the Milky Way
          as if it were Xochimilco,
          a floating garden

          and beyond it that deep
          devouring lake

as if we, too, would build
on a great Smoking Mirror

If he had killed Cortés,
left him rotting in the bush

          Moctezuma
          feared the wind
          would stop

   and leave the world

          baking in the sun
          with nothing
          to cool it.

But what of us?

          We know better.

          Cortés was not the wind!

WINDSONG

Smoking Mirror
summoned the Wind

and ordered him
to visit the Sun
                    Ollin

                    who kept so many
                    musicians in his house
                    music had vanished
                    from the earth

The Wind obeyed
and blew down the beach

raising monstrous waves
to form a bridge

                    over which he might cross
                    and return
                                        with players
                                        and their instruments

                    Ollin
                    saw him coming
                    and warned his orchestra

                              -*When the Wind speaks*
                              don't answer or you're lost!

Robed in yellow red and green
they sat in silence...

                              until the Wind

began to sing

and they couldn't help
but accompany him

VECTORS

Moctezuma
fought
his end

even   converging
as   on
he   a
assumed   particle
it   of
                        dust   snakes
Cortés   in
knew   in   the
beyond   space   bush
a   !
doubt   made   shudder
destiny   earth   at
moved   quake   the
through   news
him   birds
                        in
that   the
they   air
should
meet
like
parallel
lines

7

THE MOCTEZUMA POEMS

1 - MOCTEZUMA

He had seen the ancient drawing
of bearded men on floating islands

When at last they came he dispatched
ambassadors bearing a mask inlaid

with a turquoise serpent and a request
that they advance no further.

> His name meant,
> HE-WHO-SHOOTS-AT-THE-SKY,
> and his prayers rose like arrows

> through days of fasting
> and sacrifice

even as they marched
to Tenochititlan

> where he greeted them
> as brothers,

stood beside them
on the Palace roof

> his people hurling rocks
> and insults,
waiting patiently
for the blow to his head

that would make the whole spectacle
explode and disappear.

2 - OF HIS PHYSICAL PRESENCE

Bernal Diaz says
the great Moctezuma

> was a thin man of forty
> with golden skin,
> hair covering his ears,
> a long but cheerful face,
> a thin black beard,
> good eyes
>
> and a manner
> combining gravity
> and tenderness.

He bathed daily
had many mistresses but was free
of perversion,

> (if one discounts the rumor
> he sometimes dined
> on little boys)

He ate
behind a golden screen
surrounded by advisors

and so impressed
his Conquerors that they
doffed their caps
to him,

nodded in sympathy when
he told Cortés:

"Behold, Señor Malinche,
my body is flesh and bone,

my house, like yours,
of wood and stone and lime."

3 - AT WHAT POINT DID HE BREAK

They took Moctezuma hostage,
leading him from court
at knife point
            Vasquez
            booming the command,

            Alvarado
            holding the blade—

            but allowed servants
            to bathe him,

            ambassadors to bring
            suits and tributes.

Asked about his health
Moctezuma replied

            he found being a prisoner
            restful.

They taught him parlor games,
built a sloop to take him
sailing on Xochimilco,
held him in such
affection

their eyes grew wet
when he cried—

and, again,

years later,
recalling how his spirit broke

when Cortés
placed him in chains
then stroked him
like a lover.

4 - THE ROYAL FIFTH

On his way to Tenochtitlan
the Tlaxcalans showed Cortés
evidence of a vanished
race of giants–

a thigh bone
he measured against
his own before
shipping it to Carlos,

who stood before a mirror
in Castile
wondering what
it meant

to rule a world
of which he would remain ignorant.

5 - VANISHING POINT

Moctezuma
begged his people to accept
their fate
       but they cursed
       and stoned him.

After he lay dead
the Conquerors
fled
       on a moonless night
       (La Noche Triste)
so weighed down
with gold
       they could neither
       ride nor swim.

Many were killed

but Cortés
returned to defeat Cuauhatémoc,

whose name now
decorates
       boulevards
       banks
       and a statue

       south of Rio Panuco.

MATAMOROS

Cuauhtémoc
last Aztec Emperor
is now
a yellow statue
at the gateway of a village
on the far side
of Laguna Pueblo Viejo
just south
of Tampico
you can see him
holding a yellow spear
in a yellow hand
the royal fierceness
of his yellow face
become
a depository
for
zopilote shit!

surrounded
by a yellow mist
he appears to protest
a conquest
by men like Grijalva
who thought
the river
that bears his name
a passage to the Pacific
and mistook Indians on its banks
for Jews and Moors
because
they were dark
and had no
foreskins

CACAMATZIN'S SONG

So say I Cacamatzin
King of Texcoco

I can see my father

    Nezahualpilli

with his father

    Nezahaulcoyotl

walking arm-in-arm
as mist rolls down the mountains
and trumpets peal on a wind
from Xochimilco
that bends every stem
in a garden
full of flowers...

        on this spot
        where flutes and drums
        now fill the air,

I have watched mist and wind
congeal into armor,

felt earth tremble
like a feather necklace,

heard the quetzal raise
a shield of song
to protect itself
against rain

falling like the arrows
of an invading army.

Father
in this land of flutes
and drums
            I remember you!

THE CONCUBINE

-after "The Woman of Chalco"

Axayacatl,

in Tetzmelucan,
I rubbed pine and maguey oil
into my hands,
put on a skirt and blouse
the color of prickly pear
whose fruit inside
is sweet.

       Let me in.

I come from Xaltaplan
where we are slaves
of the Honey Bear.
Let me show you
how many ways I know
to find honey.

        What?

You say your bees
have died and your hive
is empty?

       Then I'll spin
       a cocoon
       for your caterpillar.

       No?

       You're tired of love
       and want to rest?

Poor pile of ashes,
let me bank your fire
with laughter.

Don't be afraid.
You've nothing to lose.

And one day
when I'm old
with sapless limbs

a hag among young whores,
they'll call me "Mother"
and ask me to sing
about my desire
for you

my King,

Axayacatl!

AFTER A MAYAN FOLK SONG
BY ANTONIO MEDEZ BOLIO

"A god need but breathe
into the wind

and the direction
of the wind changes."

Who knows this better
than the woman

who gives her heart
to an unhappy man.

NOTES ON A GLASS HARMONICA

News at the Hotel Flamingo:
Marvin Gaye is dead, shot
by his father. Zopilotes circle
your longue chair by the pool.
His voice in your head
sings about *sexual healing*

※

The way you like the temperature
not too close, a chill in the air.
Starlings in eaves around the patio,
are ashes on the wind. Again
this year you have survived the violence
that gives you back yourself.

※

You wanted most of the women you saw.
A kid asked you to take him across the street.
The *bruja* wore the same material as her
tablecloth. She said, "If what I tell you
Isn't true, you get your money back."

※

You finally look up. No familiar faces
at the café. The ship has gone.
This isn't France. Is not the moon.
Lemon peel floating in your cup.

※

Statues in Merida watch you pass
Their eyes expunged. A man
Pitches pennies against a wall.
You were here before, when Kukulkan
Sat in his stone case and sang:
    Tenderness without remorse…

19

ZOPILOTE AT THE HOTEL FLAMINGO

The bird had him
In its sights.

Breaking the air
with heavy wings
it alighted
still closer
on the roof
around the patio.

First
he saw himself
through its eyes
and thought:
If you weren't
alive I'd pick
your bones…

Then
he flew
back
into his own eyes

150TH ANNIVERSARY
OF MEXICAN INDEPENDENCE

Neruda thought
all Mexicans were *pistoleros*
but that the power
of Latin American poetry
was the real *pistola*
waiting to empty
the vastness of its chambers
loaded with forests
rivers and mountains
yet to be named

Vallejo knew
the Indian in him insisting
that things had names
no matter what we called them
or neglected to
that many things
we call by name
remained
undisclosed

NUTUTUN'S
fresh waters
pooling outside PALENQUE
where students from
EL DISTRITO FEDERAL
offer me *mota*
COATZACOALCOS'
flaming rigs
at night
fill the sky
with so many fiery suns
supernova exploding in the west

over LA VENTA
a womb full of Olmec heads
and fossil fuel
to drive the engines
of both AMERICAS

oil is
the sunless sea
supporting SAN ANDREAS' red roofs
the black tide cradled
beneath CATEMACO
where people eat monkey meat
as they did long ago
for the Aztec Eucharist
when it was an honor
to be skinned and cooked
to return again
as a butterfly
or a hummingbird

REFLECTIONS IN A SMOKING MIRROR

From the first
   Moctezuma feared it
and took such precautions as he could
    against the end
of his world

      Crazy Horse
     perceived
they'd all die singing or fighting
   or ambushed
     in their sleep

Only the Peace Chiefs
   among the Crow
     Cheyenne and Blackfoot decided to
      stand the slaughter
    unresisting

     in the belief
      that even the annihilation
  of their race
couldn't reduce the Great Spirit
     and might serve as a lesson
      for the minds
      of men

TIMEPIECE

What the Maya knew
was that every twenty years
   their calendars
   failed to mesh

as if the sun and moon
were gears disengaged
   on the cusp
   of life and death

where even the gods
fear a force beyond which
there is no force

    a vector
     nothing accounts for...

what else can explain
the concept of zero

    in a jungle
    where orchids spill
    in flaming abundance
    from giant mahogany

as if to say
here

   we cannot speak
   of absence

TIERRA DE NAKUK PECH
Kohun Liche

Masks
on temple walls
stare
     into space
     through eyes
like comets crossing a void

          (que misterioso es
          una inteligencia
          que no existe hoy
          en la tierra!)

      eyes
that see
and do not
     clouds
     creased by light

 like a serpent's tongue...

         what's been lost
         to a civilization
         buried in complexity

         waits for us
         at the end of deception

         the face of immensity
         whose eyes are comets
         crossing a void.

MOTHER EARTH

Quetzalcóatl
& Tezcatlipoca

descended
to find Mother Earth
a many-limbed monster
             moving over
                  water
a mouth
at the articulation
  of every limb.

             Becoming serpents
                  they twisted
and pulled her apart
to create land and sky

both of which
cried

        remembering
their origin.

        Upset,
             the gods
             tried to make
             amends
by creating men
from her unused meat,

grass
trees & flowers from her hair,

meadows full of wild spices
from her skin,

valleys

& volcanoes from her nose,

caves
from her mouth
and from her eyes
fountains and wells.

        Still,
her tears fell...

        and to this day
she refuses
to bloom or bear fruit
until
    she's slaked her thirst
    for blood

        eaten her fill
        of human hearts.

VIX A KAVA

Vacub-Hunahpu quit the court of Xibalba
After a scoreless game of pelota
Entertaining an idea

THE QUETZAL IS A STATE OF HEART
Not to be quarried in the jungle tangle
Of priests and athletes

It loves the high ground where thin men
Practice the dangerous extraction of chicle

First he waited by an inlet
Where azure and ochre ran together
Then made his way up the mountain

At twilight the upper earth is ferrous
At twilight sun has a quality of aspic
At twilight they descend from trees
With the gum that holds man's parts together

THE MYSTIC WARRIOR

From where
you sit
      Coatlique

war
is a flower
spreading its petals
over the land,

      a nuclear blossom.

Pick me
as you will.

      I am an orchid
      for your corona.

Whole galaxies
are bouquets in your hand!

      (0)
      ( )
      ( )
     ~~~~~~

.

II
MY NAME IS NAKUK PECH

In the district of Mani, in the province of Tutul-Xiu, an Indian named Ah-cambam, filling the office of Chilan, that is one who has charge of giving out the responses of the demon, told publicly that they would soon be ruled by a foreign race who would preach a God and the virtue of a wood which in their tongue he called "vahom-che," meaning a tree lifted up, of great power against the demons.

Friar Diego de Landa,
YUCATAN BEFORE AND AFTER THE CONQUEST

SYNCHRONICITY

In 1962, I drove from my sixth floor walk up on East 9th St. and Ave. B to a hotel on San Juan de Letrán in Mexico City. One evening I stopped at a bookstall where I chanced upon an UNAM Edition of <u>Crónicas de la Conquista</u>. At the counter of a restaurant, The Milky Way, I read the "Crónica de Chac Xulub Chen," by a Mayan *cacique*, Nakuk Pech, in which he recorded the Conquest of his homeland, a heart-breaking account of sub-jugation and resistance. I sat spellbound among dark faces in a white tiled room listening to a voice speak inside my head as I read words on the page. I was struck by the similarity of our names.

Nakuk Pech. Paul Pines.

But I was unprepared for the moment of his baptism, and the name he chose after his "head has been dunked under water."

Pablo Pech. Paul Pines.

Late at night, in a strange city, I heard the call of underlying symmetry, and would spend the next five years translating it.

Nakuk, who becomes Pablo, is realized in English through Paul.

In 1966, I returned to the USA after a six month voyage to Vietnam to find a country I didn't recognize. Once again I drove to Mexico, this time to Mérida, then to Progresso, and finally to an abandoned hotel on a strip of beach to the south. Over the weeks, I befriended local Mayans, and felt at home for the first time since leaving South East Asia. They reminded me of Vietnamese, the way women laughed as they plaited each other's hair. We cooked fish over an open fire. I sank into a belonging I hadn't felt before, or since. I learned that here, as in Nam, what I'd thought of as "plaiting" was a search for fleas—in Yucatec Mayan, *pech*.

I opened a map to find the name of my village: Chic-Xulub. Nakuk had lived in Chac-Xulub-Chen.

The emergence of meaningful coincidences suggests underlying symmetries as a line of white water in a tropical sea indicates a reef below the waterline. By an unknown homing device I'd inadvertently found myself in Nakuk's once proud city, now a few small huts, reading his words.

Just after the New Year, as I prepare this manuscript for publication, Face Book suggests I friend one Miguel Cocom Pech. On January 15th, 2010 I write to Miguel describing my encounter almost fifty years ago with another Pech, undoubtedly a distant relation. In May he answers, inviting me to contact him at his personal email address.

MY NAME IS NAKUK PECH

1

My name is Nakuk Pech. My descendants were the first Conquistadors of Maxtunil. My father is Ah Kom Pech, now called Don Martin, from Xulkum Cheel. Our lord, Ah Naum Pech of Motul, put us in charge and I governed the two provinces of Chichinica and Chac-Xulub-Chen. Here, in good faith, I set this down.

The Spanish settled the great city of T-Ho in the 5th division of Katun 11 Ahahu. In Ahahu 9, they introduced Christianity which they brought with them in 1511. Before the Spanish came I was prince of Chac-Xulub and remained so until Francisco Montejo appeared in 1519. When the first great Mayor, Alvarez, came to T-Ho, I was chief, and when Alvaro Caravayor came after him. Later, when Don Thomas Lopez came, I was still Nakuk Pech. But after they held my head under water I became Don Pablo Pech.

When the Spanish came to Maxtunil, home of Nachi May, we honored their captains with food and presents hoping they wouldn't go further into our land. Our fathers surrendered to them. When they returned we gave them the woman Ixnakuk to prepare their meals. Since they first set eyes on us, Maxtunil has been destroyed three times.

Fernando Cortés and Espoblaco Lara came to Cozumel for the third time on February 28, 1519 with someone who spoke our language. This is where Montejo and his men heard about

35

Chichen Itza, which they found later that year. During this period the Spanish became known as *'chupadores de anonas'*, which stuck to them for twenty years. Before they came to Chichen-tza nobody had ever eaten a custard apple.

By August 13, 1521—the year they were attacked in Cupul—they'd conquered Mexico. That same year they returned to Chichen Itza under Don Francisco Montejo to depose the war-chief Cupul. In 1542, they settled the territory of Merida and began collecting tribute. The powerful priest Kinich Kakmo--and Tutul Xiu, the King of Mani, bowed down to them. Soon other first families did likewise.

Nachi Cocom and Ah Cahout submitted to the word of God and King—surrendered their flags and coats-of-arms in behalf of the Conquest. And when Uasdi Mabum Chane learned that the true God had come he spent the rest of his life spreading the Gospel—in Mani to Tutul Xiu, west to the Cheels and beyond to the Cupuls and Nadzcab Canul. Through him, one day, the word came to my father's land, to Ah Tunal Pech.

Ah Naum Pech gathered the youth and told them: "On the day 'hun imix,' at dawn, a bearded Magus will come from the east with the word of the true God. Welcome him in certain joy." This message traveled through vine and bush as far as Nadzcab Canul: "Behold, your guest comes. Receive him eagerly."

That's what they said, and fell to their knees when Spanish ships first appeared in CanPeche waving white flags.

I was Prince Nakuk Pech when the Spanish sailed from Champoton to CanPeche and imposed the first tribute. I accompanied Ah Macan Pech, his younger brother and my father who came all the way from Xulkum Cheel, when they decreed what they wanted from the village chiefs. We saw it all. So did Nachi May who became friendly with the Spanish who slept under his roof.

After they gave us overcoats, caps, shoes and rosaries, we left together–Ah Macan Pech of Yaxkukul and my father Ah Kom Pech who was the greatest of us all. Later, when we heard they were going to T-Ho on the CanPeche road, we brought them wild turkeys, honey and delicious meals–which they craved in abundance.

Don Francisco Montejo was just and severe. He came to T-Ho first in 1541 with Francisco Bracomontes, Francisco Tamayo and Juan Pacheco y Perarberes. A year later, he began distributing villages to the Conquistadors. The scribe, Alvarez, listed the tribute owed by each village. My family and friends gave accordingly. Before they came I was chief. After they arrived in T-Ho, I and everyone in my land were given to the new lord of Chac-Xulub-Chen, Don Julien Doncel. He took my hand in front of Don Francisco Montejo. So I was handed over to Don Julian, and began collecting tribute for them, these holy men.

I was first to govern Chac-Xulub-Chen when the ancient line of Macan Pech and Ah kom Pech came to Yaxkukul, Xulkum Cheel and Maxtunil with their scribes, priests and war-chiefs. We didn't expect the Spanish, so the city was never fortified. But when I was prince, I tried to strengthen it. News of their arrival came unexpectedly from T-Ho. I determined to reconcile everyone in Chac-Xulub-Chen: I, Don Pablo Pech and my father, Don Martin, the original conquistador of Xulkum Cheel.

But the Spanish weren't like the Maya at heart. Immediately, they told us that their rule extended to the ends of the earth and demanded tribute. We who were first to pay it were knighted and given power under God and King. We were made noble, and our children also will be noble until the sun goes out. We were the top-men before there was a Holy Church, before the Spanish ruled or came together in prayer. Before I received Christ, I, Nakuk, was chief. But I accepted the Blessed Sacrament and Holy Faith, I was first to raise the flail, to instruct others in the word of God and King.

Nobody had ever seen a white man before Jeronimo Aquilar was captured in Cozumel by Ah Naub Ah Pot, which was how we learned about them before their appearance in the interior. When they came, Ah Macan Pech greeted them and I addressed the Spanish prince. They sent fifty of our top-men to Spain to serve the King's table. Aquilar discovered our land in 1517, when we marked the end of the 'katun,' with an inscription in stone. After the Spanish came, this was never done again.

I, Don Pablo, son of Don Martin, the original conquistador of Xulkum Cheel, loudly proclaim the day, month and year we welcomed our foreign lords: October 13, 1518. Don Francisco Toral, first bishop to the Maya, baptized our cities. He held our heads under water and raised aloft images of St. Paul, St. Louis, St. Anthony, St. Sebastian and St. Diego. After I received the bread and wine, he called me Pablo. Ah Naum Pech told us: "Behold, the one God has come to our shores–the true God. Go forth reverently and accept Him. If they are hungry, give them turkey, chicken, corn, honey and beans. Let Christianity enter so we may learn how to serve God."

The Spanish promised us eternal life, and the Maya listened. When they landed in Yocol-Peten, Montejo asked us in Castillian if we'd been baptized. We told him: "We don't understand." *Yu-ca-tan.* This is how the Land of Turkey and Deer got its name.

2

The Spanish went north for Mayan slaves in 1543. They needed slaves quickly. On their way they imposed a heavy tribute on Popoce. When the people gathered with turkey, honey and corn, the Spanish detained the scribe Caamal of Sisal and held him hostage for a year, during which he guided them in Zaci. The Franciscans came to Champoton in 1545, our Redeemer firmly in their hands. They baptized the scribe Caamal. After holding his head under water, they called him Juan de la Cruz because he always told the truth, and placed him at the head of Sisal where he remained in power for many years.

Sorcery stirred things up in 1546, when the land was in upheaval. Magi came from the west promoting war. After Magi Canul and Ah Caamal arrived a foreign lord and the sons of two others were found dead in Camaz. The Spanish went directly to Zaci and declared war. The Magus Caamal Tepekan of Ah Pakam was killed in Surujano, just outside Nicte. War began on November 9th and lasted a year.

We joined forces with the Spanish–I, and my father Ah Macan Pech of Yaxkukul. We went drunk on 'pinole' because everything seemed bitter and they ordered us about like masters of the earth. For six months they rode and we followed on foot. Many witnessed these events I am writing down for my children and those to come until death takes this land for its own. Until then, because of the title given me by God (who has delivered me from fear), and our great King, I do not pay tribute–nor will my sons and daughters. In 1511, before I ever saw the prow of a Spanish ship, I gave Montejo and his captains my land. I here record the events as they happened; yes, I place them here like heart beats.

Our beloved Francisco Montejo and his troops covered their horses with wool and set out for Tutul Xiu's seat in Mani. A party of Spanish visited Ah Cuat Cocom. They were driven into the Cave of Weasels where they were blinded and left to grope their way back to Mani. Not one was left with his sight. Ah Naum Pech took two of the blind men to face Ah Cuat Cocom, who claimed to know nothing about the incident because he'd been in Chichen-itza at the time. He gave my father the authority to seize those responsible and bring them back to Mani. After they questioned the people, our foreign lords went to Ah Batun Pech Cay Cheel where they gathered strength before returning to Yaxkukul. One night villagers murdered a foreign lord whose hands and feet were feeble. That night war came to the entire region.

3

In 1547, a Spanish ship foundered off Ecab and our foreign lords marched against Ek Box and his son. In 1548, The Hermit Priest introduced Christianity to Zaci. Three years later he baptized people from the Cheels to the west, Ecab and Cozumel to the north and founded the Monastery of Zaci-Sisal. Franciscans settled just beyond town. They taught us to sing Mass and Vespers, to sing with organ and flute, simply, in a way unknown to us before.

The following year Magistrate Thomas Lopez put a stop to those who set us on fire and treated us like dogs. Our King had sent him from Castile to protect us. He delegated authority in the village and set up a new tribute. We brought blankets, salt, beeswax, chiles, kidney-beans, boiled meats and jugs of wine, much as we had given them before. Under his orders, we measured off boundaries. Don Juan and Don Francisco Montejo ordered churches built in all the villages, in addition to a town square, governor's palace and an Inn for travelers. The Inn was managed by Don Juan and Don Francisco de Montejo Pech–as they were called after their heads had been held under water.

This is the story of how we received our Spanish lords. I am writing it so those to come will know how the conquest took place and the hardships we endured under the branches, vines and trees when–through our affection–they began to rule our cities.

I, Pablo Pech, was appointed to protect the town of Chac-Xulub-Chen when the slaves rebelled. After the Holy Church was built in Cumtal, we measured the boundaries to fix what was ours so that our children might remain there until the world ends. We feared being stoned or cursed by other Maya and gave ourselves to God with fear in our hearts. The King gave us power. We measured off the forests and uncultivated fields around the town so our families could maintain them without dispute and produce food for our foreign lords.

I built a stone house north of the Church. I swear this is true. And I record it here so that in days to come others can't say it belongs to them. I want to make this clear. It doesn't belong to them, but to me, Pablo Pech, son of Don Martin--the line of Don Ambrosio Pech, or Op Pech (according to the Mayan way) of Ixkil Iztam, and Don Esteban Pech who is a scribe. And I record the suffering we and the Spanish endured because of Mayans who wouldn't accept God of their own free will. I, Don Pablo Pech, ordered the people of Maxtunil to accept Him!

Julien Doncel, our leader in Chac-Xulub-Chen, instructed the chiefs to mark the boundaries of the lands they ruled. This was after Christianity was established here with our patron saint, Santiago, who now watches over the city of Don Pablo Pech.

AFTERWORD

The CRONICA DE CHAC-XULUB-CHEN is an eye-witness account of the Conquest written by the Mayan cacique Nakuk Pech. It is one of the few such documents we possess. In it, we sense the fragmentation of a once great civilization, the tensions between feudal families that had undermined it by the time the Spanish came. The end of the Mayan world had long been in the air.

When the Spanish landed with their promise of deliverance, many Mayans were ready to believe them in much the same way as those who embraced early Christianity during the decline of the Roman Empire. The difference being that in the New World the ministry was wed to military might. In his own words, Cortés "sowed the earth with corpses and crosses." Pech was among those for whom it was a conquest by conversion.

The town of Chicxulub exists today, between Progresso and Telchac Puerto, on the tip of the Yucatecan thumb. Following the shoreline, one comes to the city of CanPeche, in the province of CamPeche, both of which take their name from the Pech clan.

CAN: snake. PECH: tick. An old account states that it was the home of an idol that had a snake on its head—and on the snake's head, a tick.

The Maya love wordplay.

Nakuk's city, Chac-Xulub, means "well of the great horns."

The name of the modern village, Chicxulub, means "the horns of a cuckold."

One might say that this is a metaphor for what happened to the indigenous Maya as described by Nakuk, also known as Don Pablo Pech.

This document is one of several belonging to the Pech family pertaining to boundaries and surveys. It was written, like the others, to establish the family's titles. But that is only part of what it does. It covers the years from 1511 to 1562 and proposes to tell us what took place. Under the cover of a title document, its author, with one foot in a lost world, emerges as a deposed prince who gave up power to retain it—yet, his voice rings with the poignancy of one who has come to understand powerlessness.

Nakuk's CRONICA is a personal and cultural swan-song.

In this version of it, I've tried to capture his voice.

III
THE BELIZE NEWS

Ever since, the territory of Balize has been the subject of negotiation and contest, and to this day the people of Central America claim it as their own. It has grown by the exportation of mahogany; but, as the trees in the neighborhood have been almost all cut down, and Central America is so impoverished by wars that it offers a poor market for British goods, the place is languishing, and will probably continue to dwindle away...

John Lloyd Stephens,
INCIDENTS OF TRAVEL IN CENTRAL AMERICA, CHIAPAS
AND YUCATAN

MIRROR TRAVEL

My driver steers his air-conditioned Ford Fairlane along the road from the Robert Golson Airport to Belize City. On my last trip in 1985, the cab had bucked over pot holes crushing crabs that scurried between the Caribbean and mangrove along the Belize River. This evening, there are no crabs, or potholes. I tell my driver that I miss both.

"We still have crabs, but they are a better class." He delivers the line dead pan. "You been here before?"

"When it was British Honduras, and half the country wanted to remain in the Commonwealth, and the other to break away."

"You remember that?"

"There were two brands of cigarettes: unfiltered Colonials and Filtered Independents."

"We still smoke both." He shows me a BH ten dollar bill encased in plastic with a picture of the Queen.

As we approach the city, the scrub that used to line the highway has given way to mini-malls and a Best Western. I comment on the apparent prosperity. My cab driver shakes his head.

"Don't walk the streets of the City at night, or show money in your wallet."

We move slowly through the old part of town, past St John's Church, cross the Swing Bridge that spans the narrow harbor where the Belize River meets the sea.

Albert Street is torn up for repairs. Where the open market stood there's a concrete building with shuttered gates, no sign of the merchants selling oranges stacked in neat pyramids, or fish mongers gutting sea turtles at the rear. My driver tells me the building contains stores, like the boutique apothecary of imported scents on the corner.

The Belize City I first walked through in 1973 was a hive of sixty watt bulbs in the tropical night, a world of dark faces and Creole voices floating on shadows. I'd arrived with the smell of the South China Sea on my clothes, adrift in this backwater of open sewers, and houses nailed together from the wreckage of hurricane Hattie in 1960.

"Here we are." My driver interrupts my reverie. "The Hotel Mopan."

The hotel I remember has been absorbed by an expanded concrete façade. Vines arch over stairs leading to the entrance. A young Creole woman behind the registration desk buzzes me in. After checking into my room, I set off to buy a phone card at the Blue Bird Ice-Cream Parlor.

On Regent Street I see a sign: NOBODY HAS THE TRUTH WRITTEN ON THEIR FACE. USE A CONDOM. The AIDS statistic here is among the highest in Latin America. AIDS was not a whisper when I last walked this street.

I recognize Brodies pharmacy, Barclays Bank, and Quans General Store. Jobless young men hang on the street; some nod but most stare or turn away. Many wear jeans low, underwear showing, hats peaked at the side or back, the thug look of music-video, ghetto-USA. Others toss Rasta dreads, or wear their hair bunched under knitted caps that jettison from their heads, frozen explosions of follicular energy suggesting a domesticated wildness.

Independence in 1981 fueled visions of a new Caribbean Nation becomes a player on the world stage. While certain places experienced unregulated development through foreign investment that never trickled down to the natives, Belize City had turned into Haiti by way of Harlem.

I walk back along the sea wall, stop a few blocks from the hotel to watch kids on the other side of the bay jump off a jetty into brackish water. A red flamboyant tree rises above a garden wall. Frigate birds circle overhead.

As I sit in the fading light, images take shape in my mind as in a polished obsidian mirror—smokey at first, then clear.

CREOLE

We meet Cornelius 'pon Albert Street
    front of Majestic Theater
where hyn come aal di way fra' Placencia
    for sell fresco
        fra' wah fancy cart
(bok home dey di say
hyn jus' a li' bit crazy)
        We hail hyn
an' see di hole whey hyn two fron' teet
    dey di gone
        Once Cornelius try
take for hyn own life in Balize River
    but it too durty, mon!
        It smell too baad!
    Bok home dey di say
hyn got MACOBE
        love sickness
'cause whey dey catch up 'pon hyn
        sudging Dorea
    dey see hyn legs
dem twitch like wah spider in wah draft...
        bot hyn be mellow now
    hyn no be vexed aat aal
        hyn plot san' an stone breese
hyn take shade in di mahket like dog
    unnah di wheel a wah truck
        Aftah hyn hail we
an' say hyn motha dead
        hyn turn we a sad smile

Ted ask:
        "Why you come up here to Balize?
    Why you not home in Placencia
        catching fish?"

Cornelius say:
  "'Cause me like it here."
Den hyn look 'roun' an gi we wah riddle:
  "Why you tink di wind call
    wah HE-WIND?
  Yah, mon! Fu' true!
    'Count 'a he raise
  de ladies skirts...an he tickle dem!"

WHAT IS BURIED HERE

Belize City is built on conch shells
mahogany chips and old rum bottles.

When they dug up the streets
to install sewer lines
you found strange things
everywhere:

> Jamaican coins
> minted early
> last century,

> carved Mayan manatee bone

> a spearhead grooved
> to hunt woolly mammoth
> in the Pleistocene.

On the porch of the Hotel Mopan
we drink rumpopo
and watch

> an alcoholic entomologist
> from the British Museum
> tanked on Charger beer

> scour the lot next door
> for a rare Belizean fly

> that bypasses larval
> and sucking stages

TAKING A SHOWER AT THE HOTEL MOPAN

Remember when love
infused every object

with a music as sustained
and personal
                    as pubic hair
                    in a bar of soap

wonderful
to be alive
            in such a resonance
            ears wide open

and to say as much

to sing
            Hush,
            can you hear me
            before you wash me off!

COASTWISE ON THE FURY

We leave the pier
yellow elder blowing
by the Customs House.

Half-way down the coast
the Coxscomb Mts bleed into the sea.

> *I know the integuments*
> *of the soul are spun*
> *from images the eye*
> *records and nourishes*
> *to weave us back*
> *into the world...*

The Captain's wife
is beautiful

> *a sea-horse*
> *in short pants.*

Every man aboard
watches her disappear
into the housing.

> *her after-image*
> *dissolves in*
> *the Caribbean.*

I stare
wondering at my sadness
why she moves me
to tears.

DANGRIGA

The Maya of Santa Rosa
Wear long faces
come to town
still suffering from
a shock
        only half
        remembered

while Carib girls pace
the streets

        coal black
        in tight slacks
        hair in corn-rows

smile at me
by the River Front Hotel
where I wait for the truck
to Mango Creek,

        smile back
        and reconsider
        the conquest
        of the New World.

CROSSING THE LAGOON

Between Rum Point and Placencia

    clouds motionless
    over the Maya Mountains
    channel morning light

we might be up
in Titicaca
cradled in a volcanic bowl

    where time is palpable
    on the water's surface

    a Medusa
    gazing at herself

    held in her iris
    closing around us
    like mangrove...

        Miss Tanni

when you turn from the bow
I can see no bottom
    to your eyes

        but a depth
        in which men drown

blue holes after dark

      plankton
      turn luminous

with darting fish .   bits of wake

kiss of wing   .   a dissolving net

spread for constellations

south of the Tropic of Cancer

GEORGE, THE KING OF RUM POINT

Fertilizes his palms with turtle grass
sea-grapes curve along his shoreline
like waves about to break
back on the sea
ancient bottles hide
beneath his pier

He plays his short-wave
graphs and measures monthly rainfall
identifies boats after dark
by their running-lights

After a few rums
he may
        point out Orion
        or suggest that our species
        has reached its prominence
        on the evolutionary scale
        because we are the least
        edible of creatures

well into his cups
he'll wink and
tell you
        Mr. Crapper
        disappeared mysteriously
        after giving us the benefit
        of his invention

ask
if you're aware

        the vortex
        of a flush toilet

turns clockwise
in the northern

but counter-clockwise
  in the southern
  hemisphere

    while at earth's navel
    it goes straight down

    there's no vortex
    at all
          in Quayacil

BIRDS OF BELIZE

The Belizean national match
is called TOUCAN

almost impossible to strike
one at a time
(two can) you can

run through a box of them
trying to light the stove

whole forests to build a fire
under a pot of beans

The main road is called

THE HUMMINGBIRD HIGHWAY

on which the only hum you hear
is loose parts of your car
in the potholes

when the Prime Minister
came to Placencia late
one election year

he told the village gathered
in the hurricane shelter

> "No other country makes postage stamps
> as beautiful as ours,
> the equal of our BIRDS OF BELIZE.
> In the same way we must
> build our country on a strong foundation."

To which
a fisherman replied

"How can we build
on wah strong foundation

when di national match y' no light?
When you just strike hyn an di head
y' jus' drop off?"

🪲

Nationally and personally
loneliness is
being in the dark
with a carton of TOUCANS

🪲

Because time
is never
out of mind

the future
is a striking edge...

Sometimes,
when I need a light,
I rub my head against it
and explode.

RUM POINT SUTRA

Another rainy day,
 cobalt clouds along the peninsula
 turn sand grey.
                Bananas I bought
                last week in Mango Creek
                are turning too.
                It will be
             a challenge to eat them
                before they go black.

   Also I am out of propane
        and must dispose of fruit
             in the fridge
     I brought back
                from San Cristobal
 two weeks ago.
                            No,
 this is not a poem
     about domesticity
   unless that be the place
 one contemplates
                the implications
                of what is
                    or will become
     indigestible.
             No!
                    this is
             the song of an idiot
             who can't let go,
                a lover with a stomach ache
                    waiting for a dial tone
 No! no-
     body on the other end
        no reason to pretend the heart

is not a fruit
shriveled by
desire.
No!

this is about fire,
a Sutra
in which the senses
are sutured
like old wounds.
No pain,
but a refrain
by Blackburn
(composed three months
before
he died)

contemplating
his coffee cup,
he wrote:

EMPTY AND ALIVE!

BUITA BANAFI

There are moments
when the grieving stops,
    the dark threatening sky
    is rent
            and light
            plays on the water.

I draw a breath wondering
why I've spent
    so much time in sorrow
    for loved ones dead,
    lost or inaccessible,
    my own demise,

    the moment's incompletion...

Orphan in
an orphaned world
I lay it all
to rest.
            God's love
            is death.

AUGUSTINE'S DAUGHTER

They're calling a Dugu in Seine Bight
for Augustine's daughter
who cries all the time.

Relatives will come from Hopkins
           Monkey River
           Punta Gorda
           Barranco

           Carib towns
           as far away as Livingston
           to beat the drums
           dance

           speak-in-tongues
           as the moon
           sheds it exo-skeleton
           on the water.

They're calling a Dugu in Seine Bight
for Augustine's daughter
who can't wash
or get out of bed.

For three nights the Priestess
will pray around a secret fire

           before the men paddle to the reef
           at sunrise with offerings
           of food and rum

in behalf of Augustin's daughter
who cries

because her grandfather
has reached back
to touch her
from the other side.

THE WAY THINGS ARE

George says
there's no lumber anywhere

but Gillie
who drives for the Banana Board
tells me that between Mango Creek
and Punta Gorda
you can find enough to build
a thousand dories--
that they're giving discounts
on transportation in Cayo.

It works that way with fruits
and vegetables.

Someone says
there's no more plantains
and next morning everyone
is holding a bunch--but when
you get to town they're out
and have only eggs
for the first time in maybe
half a year.

The same holds true for
the beach after a storm

a tropical flea-market
full of turtle grass
driftwood,
fixtures torn from moorings,
nutbrown sea-hearts...
red coral
purple sea-fans
everywhere

until a low-pressure dip
puts you to sleep

and you wake to find the shore
washed clean of what it held
all week.

But there's always water
and sand

wind in the fronds,

sea-grape cresting

purpling sea-plums

Scorpio flicking its tail
at the Southern Cross

and below it

Laughing Bird Cay

VIEW FROM THE BEACH

There's been a coup
in Guatemala

Argentina
has taken the Falklands

(which they call the Malvinas)

while Britain directs an armada
into the south Atlantic

Harriers sweep the borders
of Belize

we sit on the beach
waiting
        for the planets
        to rise

        perfectly aligned
        for the first time
        in 700 years

            MARS
            JUPITER
            SATURN
            URANUS
            VENUS

        a string
        of beads pulled
        above the horizon

        by an unseen hand.

BIRDS OF BELIZE II

This is the way
old pelicans die

        blinded by salt
        that gets in their eyes
        they miss their mark
        when they dive
        and starve

        I watch one hover
        over a pig
        on the beach which
        he has clearly
        mistaken for
        a fish.

PUNTA GORDA

Backwater of bad boys and old men
blind on charcoal rum dancing

to Toots & The Maytals:

FAT POINT

where the same shoes and dollars
pass from hand to hand
as the population
paces between

                    a defunct movie house
                    and a bar full
                    of British soldiers
                    groping whores
                    from Puerto Barrios.

could anyone live in this town
who wasn't born here
where the bush tumbles
into the sea?

What happened to the guys I knew
ten years ago shooting pool
on a fly-specked table,
smoking dope and
waving at girls
from a side-street
balcony?

Xavier got fat and moved to L.A.

Rogers holes up when not playing
guitar for Missionaries.

Now a new generation has sprung
from Cat Landing

to find
        a way out

        or discover
        there's no escape
        from a place

with a name
that refutes itself.

            Punta Gorda!

gazing across Amatique Bay
while your babies suck
sweet mountain
smoke
        or mildew
        in the folds
        of your ragged skirt.

THE BELIZE NEWS

Two days
after Belizean Independence
and almost all foreign visitors
have left...
in fact
there were so many
a West Indian P.M. kept asking
where the Belizeans were
(many of whom had been reduced
to peeping through the fence).
It rained on Saturday
as the Belizean flag was raised
to a 21 gun salute
fired by a frigate
off shore
but the firework display
was scrubbed
after attempts to light it
failed
and it was clear
most of the population
had stayed home.

In Guatemala
more than a thousand
people demonstrated in front
of the National Palace
burning in effigy
the Queen
P.M. George Price
and the Union Jack
to protest the presence
of Harrier Jets
buzzing the borders

                    as tanks
          faced each other on either side.

Locally
23 year old Rolando Allen
          an apparent suicide
                    was found hanging from a tree
          in Corozal Town
          while 17 year old Philip Grahm
     drowned swimming
               in a Ladyville pond
               and Walter Tillitz
          who was serving
     a three year sentence for
          aggravated theft
          scaled the prison walls
          and disappeared.

END NOTES

REFLECTIONS IN A SMOKING MIRROR

CONFIGURATIONS OF CONQUEST: When considering the legend of Quetzalcóatl's return from the east, it is often forgotten that this god is identified with the wind. It was this identification that gave Cortés his edge. No right thinking Aztec would knowingly kill the wind.

WINDSONG: The Wind god, Ehecatl, is a manifestation of Quetzalcóatl, the 'Plumed Serpent', god of knowledge. Smoking Mirror is another name for Tezcatlipoca, god of Fate. The two often appear working together, as spirit and matter, to produce a result--here, the delivery of music to the earth.

VECTORS: The meeting of Cortés and Moctezuma is a threshold moment in world history in which we feel the underlying *intention* of events. The precognitions and synchronicities that foreshadow the fall of this civilization speak of a hidden design that haunts its remains in ways that bleed through time.

THE ROYAL FIFTH: Cortés sent the animal bone given to him by the Tlaxcalans to King Carlos, believing it to be evidence of a vanished race of giants. More likely, the bone belonged to an animal, perhaps a prehistoric one. After all, McNeish found the kind of grooved arrowheads used to hunt wooly mammoth at Golden Stream, in Belize.

MATAMOROS: 'Death to the Moors'. The origin of this place-name in the new world is in part a tribute to men like Grijalva who mistook the circumcised natives for Moors. He records this observation in his 'Itinerario de la Isla de Yucatan.' Suffice it to say, he also mistook the peninsula for an island. Of Cuauhaté-moc, we can say only that he put on the mantel of leadership under pressure, was too young to carry it and lost it all. At the end of the battle for Tenochititlan, Cortés found him cringing behind a barricade.

THE CONCUBINE: Axayacatl (1469-1481), father of Moctezuma II, successor to Moctezuma I, continued his predecessor's military policy of conquest outside the already expanded area of Aztec control. His attempt to conquer the Tarascans resulted in a crushing defeat that may, indeed, have resulted in sexual impotence.

REFLECTIONS IN A SMOKING MIRROR: The true sons of Coatlique know she renews herself in death. This underpins the decision of the pacifist vision of the Peace Chiefs who called for the renewal of the Great Mother as the force which unites all things in the medicine wheel. It is also reflected in the *amor fati* that haunts pre-conquest Mesoamerica–in the Aztec books depicting bearded men on 'floating islands,' prophecies of destruction in the Mayan 'Chilam Baalam' and the pre-Columbian legend of Kan'il from the Cuchumatanes of Guatemala in which a village youth, empowered by the volcano god, beats back an armada of armored invaders.

TIMEPIECE: The Mayan viewed time as a repetition of patterns overseen by the gods. But behind the tapestry of recurrent time, lurks the ominous embrace of undifferentiated chaos. The Greeks called it fate, moira. To the Mesoamerican, it was a specter located at the deepest stratum of the unconscious-- the disorder upon which all order depends.

TIERRA DE NAKUK PECH: The blind gaze of the masks on the temple walls of Kohunlich is the stare into infinity--a device one finds often in religious sculpture. It is the gaze of Shiva dancing on the dwarf, forgetfulness.

MOTHER EARTH: Again, the duo, spirit and matter, Quetzalcóatl and Tezcaptlipoca, effect a transformation. In the process of becoming conscious, that is, of differentiation and discrimination, there is great suffering. As in the creation myth of Genesis, serpents are the instrument for a violent separation from the uroboric womb.

VIX A KAVA: Mayan for, "What is your name?" refers to Vacub-Hunahpu, brother of Jun Hunahpu, first generation of Hero Twins in the Popol Vuh, sacred book of the Quiche Maya, who descend into the underworld to play pelota with the Lords of Xibalba. His nephews, Hunahpu and Xbalanque, outwit the Lords of Death and compel the gods to make sentient men of maize. Hunahpu becomes the sun that illuminates creation.

THE MYSTIC WARRIOR: Coatlique, "She of the skirt of snakes," bore the war god, Huitzilpochtli, who superseded her--one of the many lunar Magna Maters similarly displaced by the male solar warrior. (Sol invictus). When the Julian solar calendar was replaced the lunar one, the oracles stopped speaking. A statue nearly nine feet tall of Coatlique as the cosmic force which gives life and renews itself in death occupied a place of honor in the Aztec ceremonial center.Unearthed in Mexico City's Plaza Real in 1790, it now can be viewed in the Anthropological Museum in Chapultepec Park.

MY NAME IS NAKUK PECH

Part I

KATUN 11 AHAU: The date the Spanish arrived in the capitol of T-Ho on--July, 1541.

AHAU 9: The date the first Spaniards were sighted by the Maya on the coast--1511.

EL ADELANTADO: Francisco Montejo, authorized by the King of Spain to colonize Yucatan. Today, his name is also found on the national beer, Cerveza Montejo.

T-HO: Ancient Mayan capitol of Yucatan on which the present capitol of Merida is built.

FEBRUARY 28, 1519: Cortés found Geronimo Aquilar on Co-zumel. He'd been stranded there for nearly eight years and could speak the native language.

'CHUPADORES DE ANONAS': The Spanish were the first to consider the 'anona,' the custard-apple, a delicacy. Before that time, the Maya had never tasted one. Spanish passion for the local varieties of apples can also be found in the chronicles of Cabeza de Vaca, De Soto and Coronado.

CUPUL: A Mayan clan that remained hostile to the Spanish long after others had submitted. They ruled the eastern provinces which included Zaci, the present Valladolid.

KINICH-KAKMO: This pyramid in Izamal, one of the largest in Yucatan, is a remnant of the greatest religious center of the Early Classic Period. It is located in the province ruled by the Cheel clan and the person referred to by that name is probably a priest.

NACHI-COCOM: Head of the clan that abandoned Maya-pan to re-establish themselves in Sotuta. When the Xiu clan requested safe conduct through Sotuta on their way to sacrifice at the great well in Chichen-Itza, Nachi Cocom agreed. He hosted a banquet for Dzun Xiu and forty others. When the Xiu were in their cups, Nachi Cocom locked the doors and killed them all–ending the rivalry between their clans in 1536.

Part II

"ON THE DAY...": hun imix, is a day that carries heavy overtones of rebirth for the Maya. This speech and a later one announcing that the True God would come from the east echoes the prophecy found in the Chilam Balaam. Brinton ascribes this prophecy to a priest of the Pech clan and dates it around 1469–42 years before the first Spanish ship foundered off the coast.

PINOLE: A distillation of roasted maize.

Part III

GERONIMO AQUILAR: A survivor of the Valdivia expedition that foundered on its way from Darien to Santa Domingo in 1511. Aquilar and five others drifted for weeks before being washed up in Ecab where they were kept in coops. All of them, except for Aquilar and Gonzalo de Guerrero (who were judged too thin) were eaten at local festivities. Aguilar escaped to become a vassal of the chief of Cozumel, where he was rescued by Cortés. Guerrero married a daughter of the cacique of Chetumal, fathered a family, pierced his nose and died fighting the Spanish.

1517: Probably the Cordova expedition.

YOCOL-PETEN: YOC HAIL (upon the water) PETEN (region) = Region-on-the-water. Brinton also suggests that the Mayan response, "Ma c'ubah tan" ("We don't understand your language.") to the Spaniards might account for the modern name of the peninsula.

A PARTIAL GLOSSARY

Axacayatl: (1469-1481), Aztec emperor, successor to Moctezuma I, father of Moctezuma II.

Black Caribs: Or the Garifuna people, are descendents of slaves escaped from foundered ships who shared the island of St. Vincents with the Red Carib until the latter were annihilated. The Black Caribs migrated along the Mosquito Coast and their settlements still exist in Guatemala and Belize. They are also called the Garifuna people, after their language, Garifuna, and still practice rituals that combine African/Red Carib traditions.

Bernal Díaz del Castillo: (1492–1585) a foot soldier with Cortés who wrote an eyewitness account of the conquest, The True History of the Conquest of New Spain, He was later granted a coffee finca in Guatemala where he records what may be the first case of PTSD, in that his nightmares of the slaughter and sacrifice of his comrades on La Noche Triste made him sleep in his armor even into his eighties.

Cacmatzin: (1483–1520) king of Texcoco, son of the previous king Nezahualpilli by one of his mistresses. Cacamatzin was strangled by Spanish soldiers torturing him in an effort to get gold.

Carlos of Castile: (1500 – 1558) aka Charles V, ruler of the Holy Roman Empire from 1519 and, as Carlos I of Spain, of the Spanish Empire from 1516 until his abdication in 1556.

Coatlique: Aztec Goddess, "She of the skirt of snakes," mother of the war god, Huitzilpochtli. She is a 'tooth mother', with her necklace of skulls and her lunar power resembles that of the Hindu Kali.

Cortés: Conquistador of Mexico, whose skill as general and politician allowed him to shape the destiny of a continent and leave the land strewn "with corpses and crosses".

Cuauhtémoc: (1502 – 28 February 1525) aka One Who Descends Like An Eagle, took power at the age of 18, in 1520, as his city was being besieged by the Spanish. He was a nephew of Moctezuma II, and married to one of his daughters. After surrendering Tenochtitlan, he was tortured to reveal the rumored cache of Aztec gold. Later, Cortés killed him for allegedly plotting his murder.

Ehecatl: Wind god, a manifestation of Quetzalcoatl, the 'Plumed Serpent', law giver and god of Knowledge and the arts.

Kukulkan: The Mayan name for Quetzalcoatl.

La Malinche: (1505 – 1529), aka, Dona Marina, was one of 21 slaves given to Cortés in Tabasco, originally from a noble family, whose facility with languages allowed her to facilitate the Conquest of Mexico. She was rewarded by Cortés and remained a powerful figure, though the epithet malinche indicates a traitor or one of low moral character.

Moctezuma II: (1466 – June 1520), aka Motecuhzoma Xocoyotzin was the ninth tlatoani or ruler of Tenochtitlan, reigning from 1502 to 1520. The Spanish conquest of the Aztec Empire ended his reign.

Montejo, Francisco: Conquistador of Yucatan and founder of its capital, Merida, where his house still dominates the central plaza and zozolo.

Nezahualcoyotl: (1402-1472) the warrior/poet of Texcoco and founder of the Triple Alliance of formerly warring cities was the embodiment of the Aztec Golden Age. He set up a personal temple to an Unknown God empty of all figures and wrote poems predicting the end of the empire and "those who loved flowers" fifty years before Cortés landed in what is now Vera Cruz.

Papantzin: Beloved sister of Moctezuma II, held hostage by Cortés in his own palace.

Quetzalcóatl: aka the 'Plumed Serpent', law giver and god of knowledge and the arts who, as the snake/bird, is at home in both the roots and branches of the tree of life. He is an intermediary, a Prometheus/Christ cast out by those to whom he had come with his mysteries and cast adrift on a raft of snake. The prophecy of his return led to the worshipful entry of Cortés, who arrived at the predicted time of year.

Smoking Mirror: the volcanic lake around which were built the central cities of the Aztecs; also, another name for Tezcatlipoca, god of Fate. The name also refers to the dark mirror of highly polished obsidian.

Taxcalans: one of a number of conquered tribes forced to pay tribute to the Aztecs who allied to Cortés helped him to overthrow that empire.

Tenochtitlan: capital city of the Aztecs and home of the emperor, it was described by the Conquistador Bernal Diaz as surpassing anything in Europe, even Constantinople.

Tezcatlipoca: Aztec diety, one of the four sons of Ometeotl, he is associated with the night sky, hurricanes, the north, the earth,war and strife. His name in Nahuatl is translated as "Smoking Mirror" and alludes to his connection to obsidian, from which Mesoamerican mirrors were made and which was used for shamanic rituals. He is often seen working in tandem with Quetzalcoatl, the pair representing matter and spirit, which were felt to co-exist in a dynamic relationship.

Zochimilco: floating garden on the lake around the capital, described as a floating bouquet between the bridges and causeways that bordered the city, the flowery hem of its skirt.

Zopilote: Classic carrion, vultures that are seen everywhere in the south of Mexico, perched on fences, feasting on road-kill, or circling aloft. Their white bald heads with a sharp gold beaks above powerful black bodies, they are among the most graceful fliers, and ugliest of visage.

ABOUT THE AUTHOR

PAUL PINES grew up in Brooklyn around the corner from Ebbet's Field and passed the early 60's on the Lower East Side of New York. He shipped out as a Merchant Seaman, spending 65-66 in Vietnam, after which he drove a taxi and tended bar until he opened his jazz club The Tin Palace in 1973 the setting for his novel, *The Tin Angel* (Morrow, 1983). *Redemption* (Editions du Rocher, 1997), a second novel, is set against the genocide of Guatemalan Mayans. His memoir, *My Brother's Madness*, (Curbstone Press, 2007) explores the unfolding of intertwined lives and the nature of delusion. Pines has published seven books of poetry: *Onion, Hotel Madden Poems, Pines Songs, Breath, Adrift on Blinding Light, Taxidancing* and *Last Call at the Tin Palace*. Poems set by composer Daniel Asia appear on the Summit label. As a translator he has contributed to *Small Hours of the Night, Selected Poems of Roque Dalton*, (Curbstone, 1996); *Pyramids of Glass*, (Corona 1995); *Nicanor Parra, Antipoems: New and Selected*, (New Directions,1986). He is the editor of *Dark Times Full of Light*, the Juan Gelman tribute issue of *The Cafe Riview* (Summer, 2009). Pines lives in Glens Falls, New York, where he practices as a psychotherapist and hosts the Lake George Jazz Weekend.

For more information: http://www.paulpines.com/
http://www.tinangelopera.com/

OTHER BOOKS BY DOS MADRES PRESS

Michael Autrey - *From The Genre Of Silence* (2008)
Paul Bray - *Things Past and Things to Come* (2006), *Terrible Woods* (2008)
Jon Curley - *New Shadows* (2009)
Deborah Diemont - *The Wanderer* (2009)
Joseph Donahue - *The Copper Scroll* (2007)
Annie Finch - *Home Birth* (2004)
Norman Finkelstein - *An Assembly* (2004), *Scribe* (2009)
Gerry Grubbs - *Still Life* (2005), *Girls in Bright Dresses Dancing* (2010)
Richard Hague - *Burst, Poems Quickly* (2004)
Pauletta Hansel - *First Person* (2007), *What I Did There* (2011)
Michael Heller - *A Look at the Door with the Hinges Off* (2006),
    Earth and Cave (2006)
Michael Henson - *The Tao of Longing & The Body Geographic* (2010)
Eric Hoffman - *Life At Braintree* (2008), *The American Eye* (2011)
James Hogan - *Rue St. Jacques* (2005)
Keith Holyoak - *My Minotaur* (2010)
David M. Katz - *Claims of Home* (2011)
Burt Kimmelman - *There Are Words* (2007), *The Way We Live* (2011)
Richard Luftig - *Off The Map* (2006)
J. Morris - *The Musician, Approaching Sleep* (2006)
Robert Murphy - *Not For You Alone* (2004), *Life in the Ordovician* (2007)
Peter O'Leary - *A Mystical Theology of the Limbic Fissure* (2005)
Bea Opengart - *In The Land* (2011)
David A. Petreman - *Candlelight in Quintero - bilingual edition* (2011)
Paul Pines - *Reflections in a Smoking Mirror* (2011)
David Schloss - *Behind the Eyes* (2005)
William Schickel - *What A Woman* (2007)
Murray Shugars - *Songs My Mother Never Taught Me* (2011)
Nathan Swartzendruber - *Opaque Projectionist* (2009)
Jean Syed - *Sonnets* (2009)
Madeline Tiger - *The Atheist's Prayer* (2010)
James Tolan - *Red Walls* (2011)
Henry Weinfield - *The Tears of the Muses* (2005),
    Without Mythologies (2008), *A Wandering Aramaean* (2011)
Donald Wellman - *A North Atlantic Wall* (2010)
Tyrone Williams - *Futures, Elections* (2004), *Adventures of Pi* (2011)

www.dosmadres.com